Dr Christopher McNall is a barrister, mediator and arbitrator at 18 St John Street Chambers, Manchester. He specialises in disputes about farms (and especially tenancies under the Agricultural Holdings Act 1986) and farming, taxation (especially of agricultural land and buildings), proprietary estoppel, and Inheritance Act claims. He has advised and appeared in many leading agricultural and tax cases in courts, tribunals and arbitrations. He holds a variety of fee-paid judicial offices, including Chairperson (Principal Judge) of the Agricultural Land Tribunal for Wales / Tribiwnlys Tir Amaethyddol Cymru. He is also a member of the Arbitrator, Mediator, and Expert panels of the Agricultural Law Association's Dispute Resolution Service and a Fellow of the Agricultural Law Association. He was Consultant Editor of the 'Agricultural Holdings and Allotments' section of the latest edition of Halsbury's Laws of England and writes the 'View from the Bar' column for the Agricultural and Rural Affairs section of Practical Law. The views expressed in this book are entirely his personal views.

# A Practical Guide to the Law of Agricultural Tenancies in England and Wales
Second Edition

# A Practical Guide to the Law of Agricultural Tenancies in England and Wales
## Second Edition

Christopher McNall
MA (Oxon) DPhil (Oxon) FRSA FALA
Barrister, 18 St John Street Chambers, Manchester

Law Brief Publishing

© Christopher McNall

All rights reserved. No part of this publication may be reproduced, stored in a retrieval system, or transmitted, in any form or by any means, electronic, mechanical, photocopying, recording or otherwise, without the prior permission of the publisher.

Excerpts from judgments and statutes are Crown copyright. Any Crown Copyright material is reproduced with the permission of the Controller of OPSI and the King's Printer for Scotland. Some quotations may be licensed under the terms of the Open Government Licence (http://www.nationalarchives.gov.uk/doc/open-government-licence/version/3).

Cover image © iStockphoto.com/GTMedia

The information in this book was believed to be correct at the time of writing. All content is for information purposes only and is not intended as legal advice. No liability is accepted by either the publisher or author for any errors or omissions (whether negligent or not) that it may contain. Professional advice should always be obtained before applying any information to particular circumstances.

Published 2022 by Law Brief Publishing, an imprint of Law Brief Publishing Ltd
30 The Parks
Minehead
Somerset
TA24 8BT

www.lawbriefpublishing.com

Paperback: 978-1-914608-76-6

*To S and F*

# PREFACE

This book is an introduction to the law of agricultural tenancies[1] in England and Wales for the non-specialist legal practitioner and rural professional.[2] Given its brevity, it cannot aim to be even remotely comprehensive, nor to be any substitute for the magisterial (and lengthy) specialist practitioners' works.[3] But, even though this book is only introductory, in reading it you are taking a worthwhile step in developing your professional knowledge of this interesting and challenging field.

This book aims to be both useful and value for money. It will guide you round some of the main landmarks of the law of agricultural tenancies, especially those held under the Agricultural Holdings Act 1986 ('the 1986 Act'). Its approach is practical and not academic. Along the way, I shall point out some of the biggest pitfalls to avoid. All this, from beginning to end, should take no more than two or three uninterrupted hours of your time.

If this book does its job, it will give you enough knowledge to be able to identify an agricultural tenancy problem when you see one (not always easy), and, having done so, to know that the problem may have to be dealt with using special tools, rather than by adopting and

---

1 The first edition had no footnotes. Reluctantly departing from this self-denying ordinance, this edition will have a (judicious) few.

2 I do not deal with the law of agricultural tenancies in Scotland. For those, see Lord Gill's Agricultural Tenancies. For the law of Northern Ireland, and the special forms of land use there (such as conacre) see (for example) J C W Wylie's Irish Land Law.

3 See the Appendix.

adapting knowledge from other forms of commercial land-holding (such as business tenancies under Part II of the Landlord and Tenant Act 1954). After you have read it, you should still be able to dip into this book as and when needed to give you a quick steer as to the sort of questions you should be asking of your client (and yourself) or where to look for more detailed guidance.

As well as updating the text of the first edition,[4] including setting out some second and further thoughts, I have included some entirely new material on subjects upon which I am regularly consulted: general Notices to Quit, and Notices to Quit those given under the so-called 'Special Cases' of the Agricultural Holdings Act 1986, and dispute resolution. I shall also make some reference to recent cases.

The recognition of agricultural law as a distinct field of expertise owes much to Nigel Davis, Graham Smith, Eleanor Pinfold, and Geoff Whittaker, who created and led the Agricultural Law Association's Fellowship programme – a potent cross-disciplinary mix of law, tax, succession planning – now well into its second decade, and continuing to prosper under the direction of Alex Carson-Taylor, Mike Holland and Dr Nerys Llewellyn-Jones. Practitioners are encouraged to join the ALA, which, as well as running courses, publishes a useful quarterly Bulletin and holds an annual dinner.

I came to agricultural law entirely by chance. When still a pupil barrister, now almost 20 years ago, I was instructed to represent a dairy farmer in a dispute about the death of his herd after eating contaminated feed. Since then, I have been very fortunate in continuing to work alongside, and to learn from, many skilled fellow practitioners. Special mention goes to Oliver Wilson (who sent me

---

4 April 2019. The attentive reader, if already possessed of the first edition, will notice that the book's title has changed, so as to make the focus of this book clearer to the reader coming to it for the first time.

those first instructions) and Liz Power at Nigel Davis Solicitors, Kevin Kennedy and Maddie Dunn at Burges Salmon, Tim Russ at Roythornes, Jonathan Clifford at Thursfields, and Barry Dearing.

This book aims to state the law of England and Wales as at 1 August 2022.

*Christopher McNall*
*Lammastide 2022*

# CONTENTS

| | | |
|---|---|---|
| Chapter One | Introduction | 1 |
| Chapter Two | The Two Types of Agricultural Tenancies | 5 |
| Chapter Three | Agricultural Holdings Act 1986 | 13 |
| Chapter Four | Succession to a 1986 Act Tenancy | 41 |
| Chapter Five | Dispute Resolution | 51 |
| Appendix A | Suggested Further Reading | 59 |
| Appendix B | Useful Addresses and Contact Details | 61 |

# CHAPTER ONE

# INTRODUCTION

A significant majority (about 70%) of the land in England and Wales is agricultural land – that is to say, is land used as pasture or for the production of crops.[1]

Much of that agricultural land is tenanted. In 2020, just under half of the farms in England[2] were tenanted (being either wholly tenanted (14%) or a mixture of owned and rented land (34%). Across England and Wales, tenanted farms vary from massive moorland sprawls[3] to tiny arable patches – with everything in between. The average farm size in England is about 215 acres[4] (about 200 football pitches).

This book will principally concentrate on two aspects of the law of agricultural landlord and tenant which are regularly encountered but sometimes imperfectly understood: the recovery of possession of

---

1 The annual 'Agriculture in the UK Evidence Pack' produced by DEFRA and the Government Statistical Service is very useful. It can be found online. At the time of writing, the most recent update was October 2021.
2 In 2021, there were about 105,000 farm holdings in England, meaning about 50,000 farms which were wholly or partly tenanted. That is *a lot* of potential disputes.
3 The highest incidence of wholly tenanted farms in England (22% of farms) is in Northumberland. The lowest (12%) is Devon and Cornwall. Deep historical reasons lie behind each figure.
4 87 hectares (ha). 1 ha (= 100m x 100m = 10,000 m2) = about 2.47 acres. Hectares are metric. Acres are not (1 acre is 1 chain by 1 furlong = 10 square chains = 1/640th of a square mile). If this book succeeds in conveying only one piece of information, remember the conversion from hectares to acres. It will definitely come in useful (eg, see the calculation in the footnote below).

agricultural holdings under the Agricultural Holdings 1986 Act ('**the 1986 Act**') and the making and opposition to succession applications to agricultural tenancies under that Act.[5]

Agricultural tenancy disputes abound, fuelled by two important trends. One is that farmland is increasing in value: over the last 10 years, it has increased in value by more than gold.[6] The other is that farming tenants are getting older. In 2020 (and continuing a long trend) about 2/3rds of agricultural farmholders (both tenants and owners) were aged 55 or older. The death or retirement of a 1986 Act tenant is (at least potentially) a succession event and is thereby capable of giving rise to dispute.[7]

Resolution of many disputes does not lie with judges in the court system, but instead lies in the parallel Tribunals system – in England, the Agricultural Lands and Drainage Division of the Property Chamber of the First-tier Tribunal and, in Wales,[8] the Agricultural

---

5   With some exceptions, tenancies first granted on or before 12 July 1984 carry succession rights. There are lots of these tenancies around. 1984 is only 38 years ago. Someone who took a tenancy in June 1984 aged 21 has still not even reached the state pension age.

6   Gold is perhaps a poor comparitor because its price is far more volatile than land. Moreover, gold is now worth less than it was in 2012 (albeit following a long period of relentless growth). Many well-known firms of land agents have produced indexed figures for land values going back decades. Most are available online. An acre of prime arable land worth about £6,500 in 2012 is now worth about £9,500 (ie, about a 45% increase, or an annual return of about 4.5%).

7   The financial stakes leading a landlord to resist a succession application or to give a Notice to Quit when the opportunity arises can be enormous. If a 1986 AHT rent is about half of the rent otherwise available (eg compare about £180/acre (FBT) to £90/acre (AHT)), 87ha gives an annual opportunity cost / 'lost rent' to the landlord of £19,350. Factoring in up to two successions (say, 60 years) = £1.161m.

8   Because agriculture is devolved to the Wales Government, which, in Wales,

Land Tribunal for Wales / Tribiwnlys Tir Amaethyddol Cymru.[9] In this text, I shall refer to these as 'the Tribunal'.

Although the 1986 Act applies equally in England and Wales, the procedural rules which govern the work of the Tribunal in England (The Tribunal Procedure (First-tier Tribunal) (Property Chamber) Rules 2013: SI 2013/1169) are not the same as those in Wales (The Agricultural Lands Tribunal (Rules) Order 2007: SI 2007/3105). If you do go to a tribunal, make sure you are using the right rules.

Other important and regularly-encountered disputes in the context of the 1986 Act (such as the recovery of tenanted land for the purposes of development)[10] must be referred to arbitration.

After reforms to the 1986 Act made by the Deregulation Act 2015, some sorts of disputes (but not those in relation to Notices to Quit) which previously could only be referred to arbitration can now be referred (but only if the parties agree) to 'Third Party Determination' (TPD).[11]

Arbitrations in relation to the 1986 Act are conducted by a single arbitrator nominated (at the election of the person seeking the appointment) either by the President of RICS (ie, a surveyor from its Dispute Resolution Service), the Chairperson of the Agricultural Law Association (who will nominate a member of the ALA's Dispute Resolution Panel), or the Chairperson of the Central Association of Agricultural Valuers. The default position is that arbitrations,

---

has legislative competence. This gives rise not only to the separate devolved Wales tribunal, but also to different secondary legislation in England and Wales, for example, in relation to the 'Model Clauses': see below.

9 For addresses and other contact details, see the Appendix.
10 Special Case 'B'
11 See the Chapter on Dispute Resolution

regardless of the identity or profession of the arbitrator, are conducted under the terms of the <u>Arbitration Act 1996</u>.

In contrast, the procedure under which a 'Third Party Determination' is to be conducted is not subject to the 1996 Arbitration Act. It seems that the parties are free to agree any procedure they want.[12]

---

12 My only experience of TPD – acting as the third party – is that the parties wanted the Arbitration Act 1996 to apply. That was convenient, but not required. If so minded, I could have framed a different set of rules.

# CHAPTER TWO

# THE TWO TYPES OF AGRICULTURAL TENANCIES

Two main Acts of Parliament apply to tenanted agricultural land in England and Wales. The statutes are mutually exclusive. Any individual parcel of tenanted land is held under the terms of one statute, or the other. It cannot be held under both.

The first – and older – is the Agricultural Holdings Act 1986 ('**the 1986 Act**'). Tenancies under the 1986 Act are often called 'AHTs' ('Agricultural Holding Tenancies') or '86 Act tenancies'.

The 1986 Act is a consolidating act, and replaces – albeit in largely identical terms – the Agricultural Holdings Act 1948 ('**the 1948 Act**'). As such, reported decisions about the meaning and effect of the 1948 Act can and often are applied to disputes about the same provision in the 1986 Act. Tenancies granted as early as 1948 (but which are now subject to the 1986 Act) do still exist.[13] 1986 Act tenancies are not only common but give rise to a host of challenging technical issues.

---

13 Although natural person tenants of this vintage are now few and far between (a 21-year old in 1948 would now be 95). More commonly, one encounters AHTs granted to companies (ie, legal persons), often as a form of planning to obtain reliefs from Inheritance Tax and its predecessor taxes. So long as a company keeps up its filing requirements and remains on the Register, it does not 'die'. If you encounter this sort of scenario, seek professional advice from an accountant as to whether this antiquated tax planning is still going to work. It may not.

The later statute is the Agricultural Tenancies Act 1995 ('**the 1995 Act**'). Tenancies under the 1995 Act are often called 'FBTs' ('Farm Business Tenancies') or '95 Act tenancies'.

The 1986 Act is still in force. It was not repealed by the 1995 Act.

The 1986 Act and the 1995 Act are chalk and cheese. They could not really be more different in their content or operation.

The 1948 Act was part of the suite of socially progressive legislation introduced by the post-World War 2 Labour government which also created the NHS and the State education system. The 1948 Act was designed to improve the fairly miserable lot of tenant farmers, and as a thanks for keeping the country fed during the war.[14]

The 1986 Act (and the 1948 Act before it) is definitely 'tenant friendly', not least in conferring what often effectively amounts to lifelong security of tenure. The 1948 Act, and the 1986 Act, are each self-contained, very detailed, statutory 'Codes'. This means that the answer to most questions about 1986 Act tenancies is to be found in the 1986 Act. There is some room, but not much, for the common law.[15]

Tenancies under the 1995 Act are very different to 1986 Act tenancies. The 1995 Act, and FBTs created under it, are the product of libertarian ideas of freedom of contract. By and large, and as long as certain overarching conditions are met,[16] the 1995 Act leaves landlords

---

14 See the discussion on agricultural security in Mark Wonnacott, The History of the Law of Landlord and Tenant in England and Wales (2012), pp 159 and following.

15 An example: The notice period is to be found in the statute, but the rules about the validity of the notice in terms of accuracy etc are common law rules.

16 A valid FBT can only exist if the 'business condition' in section 1 of the 1995

and tenants to their own devices to strike whatever deal they want to, and the terms of their FBT embody that individual deal.

Unlike the 1986 Act, the 1995 Act tenant never enjoys any security of tenure over and above the term granted.[17] The 1995 Act is not really a detailed statutory code at all. It simply establishes some fairly basic ground rules. Beyond that, the parties are on their own.

This means that many problems which arise in relation to FBTs are best solved by looking to the tenancy agreement, and what it says. There are 'off-the-peg' standard form FBTs (for example, from the Royal Institute of Chartered Surveyors and the Country Landowners Association). These are often very lengthy and detailed with sophisticated provisions for all sorts of contingencies of varying likelihoods. However, because no tenancy agreement can ever deal with every possible eventuality, or be completely comprehensive, if you have an FBT problem and the answer is not in the tenancy agreement, then you are in the undesirable position of having to imply terms (if you can) for example by way of necessity or business efficacy.[18] But, going to court to imply a term into an FBT is not the most enticing prospect.

---

Act is met (land farmed for the purpose of a trade or business), as well as either the 'agriculture condition' (the character of the tenancy is primarily or wholly agricultural) or the 'notice condition' (on or before the start of the tenancy, the parties gave each other written notice that the tenancy was to be an FBT): see, further, below.

17 An FBT for a fixed term of up to 2 years does not need to be terminated by notice.

18 See the Supreme Court's decision in *Marks and Spencer plc v BNP Paribas* [2015] UKSC 72.

## Which Act applies?

The best way of telling which Act applies is to look at the date on which the tenancy was first granted. If it was first granted on or after **1 September 1995** (the date on which the 1995 Act came into force) it cannot (except in certain unusual circumstances – see below) be a tenancy under the 1986 Act.

**1 September 1995.** Remember the date!

If you want to stop reading here, you have already justified your financial outlay in this book.

If a tenancy was first granted on or after 2 September 1995, then you are probably in 1995 Act territory and so probably do not need to trouble yourself with the intricacies of the 1986 Act.

Note the 'probablies'. There are some wrinkles. It is possible for a tenancy to be an AHT even if granted (NB, not first granted) after 1 September 1995. A good example of this would be a 1986 Act succession tenancy granted in (say) 1999[19] or obtained by virtue of a direction of the Tribunal.[20]

---

[19] See section 4(1)(d) of the 1995 Act which permits the post 1 September 1995 creation of a 1986 Act tenancy where it 'is granted on an agreed succession by a written contract of tenancy indicating (in whatever terms) that Part IV of the 1986 Act is to apply in relation to the tenancy'.

[20] ATA 1995 Section 4(1)(b). Sections 4(1)(a)-(g) set out the full list of exceptions.

## 1995 Act Tenancies / FBTs

Tenancies under the <u>Agricultural Tenancies Act 1995</u> are Farm Business Tenancies ('FBT's) but are often known just as '95 Act' tenancies.

FBTs differ from 1986 Act tenancies in a number of very important ways. An FBT gives no security of tenure beyond that provided for in the tenancy agreement, and an FBT does not create or give rise to any succession rights.

In order to be an FBT, the tenancy must meet certain statutory conditions. These are the 'Business Condition' and either the 'Agriculture Condition' or the 'Notice Condition'.

The 'Business Condition' is that all or part of the land is farmed for the purposes of a trade or business at the beginning of the tenancy, and some part remains so used at all times. The 1995 Act does not define 'farming'. Farming may or may not be the same as 'used for agriculture'.

The 'Agriculture Condition' is that, having regard to the terms of the tenancy, the use of the land, the nature or any commercial activities carried out on it, and any other relevant circumstances, the nature of the tenancy is wholly or primarily agricultural.

The 'Notice Condition' is that the parties have served on each other, at the commencement of the tenancy, written notices specifying that the tenancy shall remain an FBT even if the user of the land ceases, at some later date, to be primarily agricultural.

The Agricultural and Notice Conditions are designed to address different scenarios. The Agricultural Condition is suitable where, at the time the tenancy is granted, no substantial diversification from agricultural user is anticipated. Where the Notice Condition is met, the tenancy as granted remains an FBT, irrespective of whether the tenant changes the nature of his activity on the land from agriculture to something else. The Notice Condition therefore protects the landlord from an FBT 'changing code' because of a diversification into non-agricultural use, capable of turning the FBT into a business tenancy under the Landlord and Tenant Act 1954. That would be undesirable for a landlord since the 1954 Act would confer much greater security of tenure on the tenant than an FBT. For that very reason, in practice, the Notice Condition is almost universally complied with by prudent landlords.

Any tenancy of agricultural land first granted on or after 1st September 1995 which meets the statutory conditions for an FBT will be (and, if the Notice Condition is met, will *remain*) an FBT (and not a 1986 Act tenancy) unless it falls within one of the exceptions set out in section 4 of the 1995 Act.

The main exceptions are (i) succession tenancies (whether on the tenant's death or retirement) granted by the Tribunal under the 1986 Act; (ii) tenancies granted in writing on an agreed succession with the tenancy agreement indicating that the 1986 Act is to apply; and (iii) tenancies granted to an existing tenant over the whole or substantially the whole of land already comprised in the holding, already held under a tenancy in relation to which the 1986 Act applied, and containing a clear statement that the 1986 Act is to apply to them.

It is clear that it is made (deliberately) difficult to create a 1986 Act tenancy today. For better or worse, this significantly reduces the possibility of accidentally creating one.

But there is a parallel problem, which is losing rights under the 1986 Act, without realising it, when things are done which have the effect of bringing about an implied surrender and regrant (surrender by operation of law) which can 'use up' a succession. Examples include adding a tenant to the tenancy, and adding land to the tenancy.

1995 Act Tenancies granted for a term of two years or less expire automatically, by effluxion of time: AHA 1995 section 5.

Tenancies for more than 2 years require service of a written notice (expiring on the term date) at least 12 months before the term date. There is no prescribed form of notice. If the FBT is granted as a fixed term of more than two years, then it can only be brought to an end by such a notice to quit. If no notice to quit is given, then the FBT will continue as a periodic tenancy (from year to year) until terminated by at least 12 months' notice expiring on an anniversary of the term date.

## **1986 Act tenancies**

I have already drawn attention to 1 September 1995. Anything first granted before then cannot possibly be an FBT, but, if a tenancy, is likely to be an AHT.

The second very important date to remember is **12 July 1984**. Any 1986 Act tenancy first granted before **12 July 1984** will be a 1986 Act tenancy which will, by default,[21] carry succession rights.

Any 1986 Act tenancy first granted between 12 July 1984 and 31 August 1995 will be governed by the 1986 Act, but with some watering down. These tenancies are secure for the original tenant, but generally do <u>not</u> carry any succession rights. For those tenancies which have them, the existence of succession rights does not mean that there will actually be a succession. 'Succession rights' simply mean that an 'eligible' and 'suitable' (each as defined) aspirant successor, on the death or retirement of the tenant, may (if the landlord agrees) be

---

21 That is, regardless of whether a written tenancy agreement makes any reference to them.

granted a succession tenancy[22] or (if the landlord does not agree) apply to the Tribunal for a succession tenancy.

The succession process (ie the vesting of an existing tenancy in a successor tenant) can happen up to twice – from the original tenant to first successor (succession 1) and from the first successor to the second successor (succession 2).

The 1986 Act sets out statutory tests to determine whether someone is 'eligible' and 'suitable'.

Bearing in mind that the original tenant themselves may well enjoy lifelong security of tenure, then extending that prospect not only to successor one but also, in due course, to successor two could potentially mean a tenancy lasting for three lifetimes – perhaps well over a century. I have encountered tenancies granted in the 1950s where the tenancy is still in the hands of the original (natural person) tenant.

So, the economic impact of a 1986 Act tenancy with succession rights can be dramatic. It is generally understood that the rent of an AHT carrying succession rights is less than the rent for an FBT, and that the presence of an AHT exerts a depressing effect on Open Market Value (OMV). In financial terms, over three generations, and decades, this can be significant.[23]

---

22 Which, even though granted after 1 September 1995, will not be an FBT but will be an AHA, because one of the exceptions created by section 4 of the 1995 Act.

23 See my rough-and-ready calculation above. The obvious corollary is that an aspirant successor could, if so minded, seek to ransom the landlord, who might prefer to buy off a succession, in exchange for a long FBT, rather than risk the Tribunal directing a succession tenancy (especially if it is a first succession with a prospective second successor already on the scene).

# CHAPTER THREE

# AGRICULTURAL HOLDINGS ACT 1986

## The statutory requirements

There are three statutory requirements for a 1986 Act tenancy.

Firstly, there has to be *'a contract of tenancy'*: section 1(1). In many cases this is easy to answer because the tenancy agreement is in writing (frequently using standard forms such as those provided by the Estates Gazette). But the 1986 Act does not require an AHT to be made by a deed, or even to be in writing. Many AHTs are annual tenancies, and as such (being tenancies for less than a term of three years) are exempt from the usual formality requirements for leases: LPA 1925 section 54(2).

Valid AHTs can be – and often are – created orally (but remember – happening on or before 1 September 1995), just so long as the usual requirements for a binding contract are met: (i) an intention to create legal relations (family arrangements and 'gentlemen's agreements' may fail to satisfy this requirement); (ii) offer and matching acceptance; and (iii) consideration. It is also possible – although quite unusual – for a tenancy (which is just a type of contract) to be created (like any contract) by conduct – the consensual assumption of exclusive possession, coupled with the payment and receipt of rent of some kind.

Where a tenancy is oral, or concluded by conduct, or even in writing, the 1986 Act contains a mechanism for the implication of an extensive series of terms: see the discussion below about the 'Model Clauses' and section 7.

Section 2 of the 1986 Act can sometimes engage. This section is a sort of 'statutory magic' which converts certain non-gratuitous licences and other arrangements (whether in writing or not) which were in existence on 1 September 1995 into fully-fledged 1986 Act tenancies, *where the circumstances are such that if [the occupant's] interest were a tenancy from year to year he would in respect of that land be the tenant of an agricultural holding*'. Interests of this nature are sometimes known as 'section 2 tenancies'. They are valid AHTs, but do not carry succession rights because they are deemed to have first come into existence on 1 September 1995.

For section 2 to operate, there still needs to be (i) an intention to create legal relations, (ii) exclusive occupation (meaning, at least, exclusive occupation for agricultural purposes, bearing in mind that fields, unlike rooms, do not have doors and windows which can be locked); and (iii) some consideration, although the requisite consideration need not be monetary, but can be something of value, such as keeping the land in good heart (Mitton v Farrow [1986] 2 EGLR 1) or agreeing to reseed after harvest (Davies v Davies [2002] EWCA Civ 1791). There are exceptions to section 2. For example, it expressly does not operate to convert grazing or mowing agreements 'during some specified period of the year' into agricultural tenancies: section 2(3).

Difficult questions can arise as to whether (for example) a series of 11-month grazing licences, first starting before 1 September 1995, and where the occupant has been in continuous occupation, have given rise to a section 2 tenancy.[24]

---

24 Instances of long occupation where the occupant is hazy as to the precise date on which they first went into occupation, except that it was 'some time

The second requirement for an agricultural tenancy is that the land has to be *'let for use as agricultural land'*: section 1(2).

*'Agriculture'* includes:

> *'horticulture, fruit growing, seed growing, dairy farming and livestock breeding and keeping, the use of land as grazing land, meadow land, osier land, market gardens and nursery grounds, and use of land for woodlands where that use is ancillary to the farming of land for other agricultural purposes'*: section 96(1)

This is not an exhaustive definition. For example, it does not include the growing of wheat, which is an extremely common agricultural activity and which is undoubtedly agricultural activity within the proper meaning and effect of the 1986 Act.

> *'Livestock'* includes *'any creature kept for the production of food, wool, skins, or fur or for the purpose of its use in the farming of land or the carrying on in relation to land of any agricultural activity'.*

The courts have interpreted this as ruling out, from being AHTs, instances where the agricultural activity consists of things such as pheasant rearing for sport and the keeping of horses (unless they are being kept to be eaten or to draw the plough, either of which would qualify the horse as 'livestock').

Whether equestrian activity is a qualifying activity for an AHT can still be a grey area. In cases like Rutherford v Maurer [1962] 1 QB 16, it has been held that tenanted land used for grazing (an agricultural purpose) by horses (not livestock) in connection with a livery business or riding school (a business, but not an agricultural business) is an agricultural holding within the meaning of the 1986 Act. But there are other cases where equine use has not given rise to an AHA: seek

---

in the summer of 1995', call for particularly anxious scrutiny.

specialist advice.

The third statutory requirement is that the land used for agriculture must be *'so used for the purposes of a trade or business'*: section 1(4). Whether activity is a trade or business for this purpose can be a matter of fact and degree, especially when the business activity is quite modest (for example, the use of land to produce and sell a grass crop for an annual income of a few hundred pounds, or the keeping of a few hens to sell eggs to the local shop or at the gate) and/or is not conducted on conventional business principles (for example, where it is more akin to a hobby). There can be difficult cases – for example, use of land as a community free farm has been held not to have given rise to an AHA (Secretary of State for Transport v Jenkins (1997) 79 P&CR 118): again, seek specialist advice.

## The 'Model Clauses': section 7

Section 7 of the 1986 Act incorporates the so-called 'Model Clauses' into all AHTs, whether written or oral. The 'model clauses' concern the maintenance, repair and insurance of fixed equipment. Fixed equipment includes any building or structure affixed to the land, and any works on, in, over or under land – for example, the farmhouse and farm buildings, water and drainage systems, and gas, electrical and safety detection systems.

The model clauses are incorporated *'except insofar as they would impose on one of the parties to an agreement in writing a liability which under the agreement is imposed on the other'*. This means that the liabilities contemplated by the model clauses will apply unless the parties have agreed, in writing, something different. They apply without modification to all oral tenancies.

The full text of the model clauses is to be found in The Agriculture (Model Clauses for Fixed Equipment) (England) Regulations 2015 SI

2015/950 (England only) and the Agriculture (Model Clauses for Fixed Equipment) (Wales) Regulations 2019 SI 2019/1279 (W 223) (Wales only). The Agriculture (Maintenance, Repair, and Insurance of Fixed Equipment) Regulations 1973 are now repealed in their entirety.[25]

The English and Welsh Regulations are both extremely detailed codes which allocate liabilities for maintaining and repairing a whole range of fixed equipment on either the landlord or the tenant, and also regulate the amounts which can be claimed.

So, if the agreement lacks detail, and you want to know who (for example) has to pay to fix the smoke detector system in the milking parlour, the Regulations should provide the answer.

### Schedule 1: Matters for which provision should be made

In addition to the model clauses incorporated by virtue of section 7, Schedule 1 of the 1986 Act sets out a list of nine *'Matters for which provision is to be made in written tenancy agreements'*.

Schedule 1 applies to all tenancy agreements, whether written or oral. Some of these nine matters are obvious (and one would expect to see them in any written agreement): such as 'the term or terms for which the holding or different parts of it is or are agreed to be let' and 'the rent reserved and the dates on which it is payable'. The most important item on the Schedule 1 list regularly encountered in practice is Paragraph 9: 'a covenant by the tenant not to assign, sub-let or part with possession of the holding or any part of it without the landlord's consent in writing': see below.

If the tenancy agreement – whether written or oral – fails to make

---

[25] A change from the first edition, where they were still in force in Wales.

provision for one or more of the matters in Schedule 1, and if the landlord and tenant cannot agree what provision should be made, then section 6 of the 1986 Act gives a mechanism for resolution. This is a process which begins with the giving of a so-called 'section 6 notice', by either the landlord or the tenant, to the other, requesting that the other enter into an agreement in writing embodying all the terms of the tenancy and all the Schedule 1 matters, and, in default of which, that the matter be referred to arbitration or TPD.

So, Schedule 1 (unlike the Model Clauses) does not actually give an answer to *what* the clause should be – it just gives the mechanism for the arbitrator / TPD to decide what the clause should be.

## Assignment of a 1986 Act tenancy

Even though a 1986 Act tenancy is capable of conferring, in reality, what can amount to lifelong security of tenure on the tenant, this is not absolute. In relation to pre-July 1984 AHTs, the landlord may resist any succession application made when the tenant dies or retires.

The obvious way for the tenant to try to forestall this scenario is an inter vivos assignment (ie, an assignment when still alive).[26] Assignment by a natural person (who will eventually die) to a legal person such as a company (which, as long as it remains on the Register, may live for ever) is one way of trying to keep the tenancy alive. Assignments by natural persons to limited companies are frequently encountered, but are not free from risk. It must be borne in mind that,

---

26 You cannot effectively assign an AHA by will because a will is an ambulatory document which takes effect only at the moment of death; at which self-same moment the testator's estate has vested in their personal representatives. Nemo dat.

if the assignee company is itself to be the tenant, and to have the benefit of a 1986 Act tenancy, then the assignee company *itself* needs to continue to satisfy the statutory conditions for the existence of a valid AHA tenancy, including occupying the land itself for the purposes of a trade or business. Hence, 'dormant' or non-trading companies, or companies which undertake non-agricultural activity (such as a B and B; glamping; holiday lets; agro-tourism) may fail to satisfy section 1(4) of the 1986 Act, thereby losing the protection of the 1986 Act – an unintended and undesirable outcome.[27]

Most written tenancy agreements contain an anti-assignment covenant. The covenant often implied into commercial leases (that is, leases under the Landlord and Tenant Act 1954) that the landlord cannot unreasonably withhold consent to assignment is not implied into tenancies of agricultural holdings. As such, assignment without consent in breach of an express anti-assignment covenant in the lease is a dangerous step to take. It risks being treated as an irremediable breach of the lease, materially prejudicing the landlord's reversion, and thereby potentially giving the landlord scope to bring a 'Case E' Notice to Quit.

Where the tenancy (whether oral or in writing) is silent as to whether the tenant can assign, then there is a possibility of assignment (because all tenants have the common law right to assign).

The possibility of assignment by the tenant of their interest to a legal person (or to a much younger natural person) presents a real hazard for the landlord otherwise hoping to recover possession on the tenant's death (where there are no succession rights), or to object to a

---

[27] Non-agricultural use / diversification scenarios sometimes entice the well-heeled and ambitious landlord to seek a declaration that the tenancy is no longer within the 1986 Act. Although such claims are superficially attractive, remember that the only iron law of litigation is the law of unintended consequences.

succession application (where there are succession rights).

The 1986 Act throws a lifeline to the landlord of a tenancy without an express prohibition on assignment. Where the agreement (whether oral or written) fails to make any provision for the matter in Schedule 1 Paragraph 9, namely 'a covenant by the tenant not to assign, sub-let or part with possession of the holding or any part of it without the landlord's consent in writing' then the landlord can request (which need not be in writing, but which prudently should be) that the tenant enter into a written agreement *'embodying all the terms of the tenancy and containing provision for all of the said matters'*, and, in the absence of such agreement, that the terms of the tenancy should be referred to arbitration or third party determination.

Once a section 6 notice has been given by a landlord, it carries the very important consequence of preventing the tenant from assigning, sub-letting or parting with possession, of the whole or any part, without the landlord's consent in writing, *'during the period while the determination of the terms of the tenancy is pending'*: section 6(5). Any such transaction is void.

The same does not apply where the section 6 notice is given by the tenant. That is to say, a tenant's notice does not impose a standstill on assignment.

Therefore, a sensible landlord who faces an occupant who is or may be a 1986 Act tenant, where the tenancy is oral, or is in writing but without any anti-assignment clause, should give urgent consideration to the making of a section 6 request (ideally, by giving a written notice) so as to prevent any valid or effective assignment by the tenant.

Only the party making the original request can demand arbitration. But the 1986 Act does not give any timescale within which an arbitrator should be appointed. This gives rise to an unresolved legal question whether section 6 notices, if not consummated by the appointment of an arbitrator, expire automatically through effluxion of time (the absence to pursue the notice being treated as a sort of waiver). This has not yet been decided, and well-informed opinion is divided. Some landlords periodically issue new section 6 notices, all without prejudice to the force, meaning, effect, and validity of any previous section 6 notices, but nonetheless do not then go on to demand arbitration (which only the giver of the notice may do), therefore imposing, in reality, a permanent embargo on assignment.

If there is an arbitration as to the matters under Schedule 1 then the arbitrator cannot rewrite the tenancy agreement ad lib. Her power is limited to specifying the existing terms of the tenancy, and making provision for the Schedule 1 matters only where it is 'reasonable and just' to do so.

## Recovering possession of a 1986 Act tenancy: Types of Notices to Quit

1986 Act tenancies do not expire by effluxion of time. Even death does not bring them to an end, since the benefit of the tenancy vests in the tenant's personal representatives.

A key feature of 1986 Act tenancies is that the tenant's security of tenure is achieved by the imposition of restrictions on landlord's notices to quit and the conditions which must apply for them to be given.

The recovery of possession of land held under a 1986 Act tenancy can be complex, difficult, and time-consuming. It is full of traps for the unwary.

The recovery of possession under the 1986 Act is mainly a 'notice based' system. This means that even when the tenant is in clear breach of a statutory or contractual obligation (for instance, the obligation to pay rent as and when due) that breach, in and of itself, is not sufficient to allow the landlord to bring a Notice to Quit or to recover possession. The landlord must, in most instances, give a written notice of some kind. Under the 1986 Act, it is the giving of the right notice at the right time in the right way which entitles the landlord to recover possession – and not the underlying breach itself.

There are two main kinds of notice to quit AHTs, and they are governed by different rules.

The first is a 'general' notice to quit (sometimes called an 'unqualified' notice). A general notice does not need to give any reason for wishing to recover possession (although it may) but it must be valid at common law (i.e., it must be sufficiently clear, unambiguous and precise: see Mannai Investment v Eagle Star [1995] 1 WLR 1508).[28] Usually (but not always) at least 12-months' notice (expiring on a term date) is required, even if the tenancy agreement says that less than 12 months notice is needed: section 25(1).

The second kind of notice to quit is a 'Special Case' notice. That is a notice which seeks to rely on one of the 'Special Cases' set out in Schedule 3 of the 1986 Act.

---

28 But the notice need not be addressed to the right person, if (applying *Mannai*) the reasonable recipient would have considered the notice to be meant for whoever was actually the tenant and would not have been misled. So, in *Turner v Thomas* [2022] EWHC 1239 (Ch), Zacaroli J upheld a notice to quit addressed to X, a natural person, who (unknown to the landlord) had assigned the tenancy to Y, a company of which X was sole director, shareholder, and secretary. In July 2022, the Court of Appeal granted the landlord permission to appeal.

| Case A | Smallholding termination provisions |
| --- | --- |
| Case B | Non-agricultural use for which planning permission has been granted |
| Case C | The Tribunal has awarded a certificate of bad husbandry |
| Case D | Non-compliance with a Notice to Pay Rent or a Notice to Remedy a breach of the tenancy |
| Case E | The tenant has committed an irremediable breach which materially prejudices the landlord |
| Case F | Tenant is insolvent |
| Case G | Death of tenant |
| Case H | Ministry tenancy |

If a Special Case notice is to be given, it is particularly important to pay close attention to the wording of the Special Case and to get the notice right.

There is no restriction on the type or number of notices to quit that a landlord can give at one time. A landlord can give a general notice to quit alongside one (or more) Special Case notices. The giving of a Special Case notice under one case does not preclude the giving of a Special Case notice under another case. Notices are often given expressly without prejudice to the force, validity, meaning and effect of any other notices. 1986 Act notices can also be given expressly without prejudice to the contention that no 1986 Act tenancy in fact exists (for example, if it is considered that the tenancy has already come to an end for some reason, or if the evidence supporting the existence of a 1986 Act tenancy at all is thin,[29] or non-existent).[30]

## **Bringing and challenging a 'general' Notice to Quit**

A valid Notice to Quit ends the tenancy.

However, section 26(1) of the 1986 Act gives the tenant a crucial safeguard. Where a general notice to quit is given and "*not later than one month from the giving of the notice to quit the tenant serves on the landlord a counter-notice in writing requiring that this subsection shall not apply to the notice to quit*" then (subject to s 26(2)) the notice to quit shall not have effect unless, on an application by the landlord, the Tribunal consents to its operation.

For a tenant receiving a general notice to quit, **speed is of the essence!** In responding to a general notice to quit, the tenant's counter-notice must be served within one month from the giving of the notice to quit. This is a rigid and inflexible time limit. The Tribunal does not have any power or discretion to extend the time limit for the tenant's counter-notice. If the tenant fails to give a counter-notice in time, then the Tribunal will have no part to play, the general Notice to Quit

---

[29] For example, where there is doubt as to whether the occupant was first in occupation before or after 1 September 1995.

[30] The so-called 'Grammer v Lane' basis.

becomes 'incontestable', and (unless it is subsequently found by the Court to be invalid for some reason at common law, e.g. for vagueness, or because it expires on the wrong day) it will bring the tenancy to an end.

There is no prescribed form which the tenant's counter-notice should take. It can be as simple as a letter, but it must make clear that the tenant proposes to rely on section 26 and wishes to refer the general notice to quit to the Tribunal.

If the tenant does give a counter-notice, in time, then the general notice to quit is not effective unless and until the landlord applies to the Tribunal (within a specified timeframe, but which can be extended by the Tribunal) and the Tribunal consents to the operation of the Notice to Quit. If the landlord does not make such an application, and/or is not in time and the Tribunal refuses to extend time, then the notice to quit loses its effect.

If making an application to the Tribunal, the landlord then faces two further hurdles.

The first is that the Tribunal will only give consent if the landlord satisfies the Tribunal that one or more of the six statutory grounds (set out in section 27) for the recovery of possession applies. These are (a) 'good husbandry'; (b) 'sound management of the estate'; (c) 'agricultural research or education, or for the purposes of the enactments relating to smallholdings'; (d) 'a purpose desirable for the enactments relating to allotments'; (e) 'greater hardship would be caused by withholding than by giving consent'; and (f) 'the landlord proposes to terminate the tenancy for a non-agricultural purpose'.

None of these grounds are entirely straightforward for the landlord to establish. Unless the landlord is aiming for the long shot that something will go wrong at the tenant's end so that the tenant fails to give a counter-notice in time, then the landlord must think ahead as to whether it will be able to demonstrate to the Tribunal that it genuinely meets one of the section 27 gateways (in relation to which the landlord bears the burden). If the answer to that is negative, or is in doubt, then referring the notice to the Tribunal is likely to be a waste of time and (the landlord's) money.

The second obstacle is that, even if the landlord does succeed in establishing one of the section 27 grounds, the Tribunal still has a discretion as to whether it gives its consent: the Tribunal must (not 'may') withhold consent to operation of the notice to quit if satisfied that 'in all the circumstances it appears to them that a fair and reasonable landlord would not insist on possession'. That is obviously a fact-sensitive decision. The 1986 Act does not give any further guidance, and nor do the reported cases.

It is technically possible (although in reality unlikely) that a Tribunal could consider that greater hardship would be caused to the landlord by withholding consent than to the tenant by giving consent (one of the section 27 gateways: a subjective test) but nonetheless still consider that a fair and reasonable landlord would still not insist on possession (an objective test), meaning that the Tribunal would not consent to the operation of the general Notice to Quit.

If a notice to quit is of the kind where a challenge, under the terms of the 1986 Act, has to be referred to arbitration, and arbitration is demanded, then the notice must be referred to arbitration. The Tribunal will have no role at all. There is no prescribed form for a demand for arbitration, but it must be in writing and must make clear that the tenant disputes the validity of the reason(s) given in the Notice to Quit, and demands arbitration.

Like a counter-notice, the tenant's demand for arbitration is also subject to a strict, non-extensible, time limit. It must be served on the landlord 'within one month' of the service of the relevant notice: <u>The</u>

Agricultural Holdings (Arbitration of Notices) Order 1987 SI 1987 /710 (which sets out this, and many other important, time limits for arbitration).

The following Special Cases go to arbitration and not the Tribunal:

- Cases A, B, D, and E.

    The following Special Cases go to the Tribunal and not to arbitration:

- Cases C, G.

    The arbitrator will make an award upholding or dismissing the Notice to Quit. An arbitral award upholding the Notice to Quit is not an order for possession. If the tenant does not vacate, then the landlord will have to bring possession proceedings in the County Court.

    If the Notice to Quit is referred to arbitration, and the tenant loses, the tenant can nonetheless perhaps still seek to challenge the validity of the Notice to Quit in court, for example by way of an arbitration appeal[31] and/or by defending possession proceedings on the ground that the Notice to Quit is vague or ambiguous.[32] Whether such rear-guard action is sensible or

---

31 If the parties to the arbitration have not agreed to exclude appeal rights, and some error of law or serious procedural irregularity giving rise to injustice can be identified: see Arbitration Act 1996 sections 67-69.

32 In *Windsor-Clive v Rees* [2021] EWHC 3180 (Ch), HHJ Jarman QC dismissed a counterclaim by the tenant (brought in response to a Case B Notice to Quit which had been upheld at arbitration and on appeal to the High Court and which was then the basis for a claim for possession) that he was, regardless of the valid and unappealable Notice to Quit, the beneficiary of a form of equity in the tenanted land arising from alleged representations

worthwhile is a matter for the tenant.

## Bringing and challenging a 'Special Case' Notice to Quit

### Case A: Smallholdings

There are five requirements to a successful Case A Notice to Quit, which must all be satisfied:

i. A smallholding under Agriculture Act 1970; and

ii. Let after 12th September 1984; and

iii. The Tenant is over 65; and

iv. Suitable alternative living accommodation is available; and

v. The tenancy agreement contains a statement that Case A shall apply.

Case A is not frequently met since it is available only to local authority landlords who have smallholding estates ('county farms estates') within the meaning of the Agriculture Act 1970. Although these smallholdings were intended as 'starter farms', some smallholders did not move on to larger farms and remain in possession decades later.

The tenant's challenge to a Case A Notice to Quit begins with a 'Demand for Arbitration'. There is no prescribed form for this, but it must be in writing and must make clear that the tenant disputes the validity of the reason(s) given in the Notice to Quit, and demands arbitration. This demand must be given within one month of service

---

decades earlier that he would not be required to leave the holding without 'fair compensation'.

of the notice to quit. If that is not done, then the Notice to Quit cannot be challenged at arbitration.

## Case B: Development

**The land is required for use, other than agriculture, for which actual or deemed planning permission has been granted and that fact is stated in the Notice.**

Case B can be used in relation to the whole holding, or (but only in certain circumstances)[33] part of the holding.

Case B can also allow the landlord to give 'short' notice (i.e., less than the 12 months expiring on a term date which the 1986 Act otherwise requires) but only where it is given in pursuance of a provision of the contract of tenancy which authorises the resumption of possession of the holding or some part for some specified purpose other than the use of land for agriculture.[34]

If the Notice is challenged (which is by way of a demand for arbitration: see above), then it is important that the landlord can prove (albeit, in the event of dispute, only to the appropriate civil standard, ie, the balance of probabilities) that she satisfies all the elements of Case B.

There are many reported decisions on the meaning and operation of Case B Notices. Although some general principles can be stated, these

---

[33] Where there is a written tenancy agreement which authorises the resumption of possession of part; where part of the land is needed for the purposes set out in section 31 of the 1986 Act; or where the reversion of the part required has been severed: seek specialist advice.

[34] AHA 1986 section 25(2)(b). This obviously will not work where there is no written tenancy agreement.

are still potentially subject to challenge and argument.

'Required' means that the landlord must have a genuine and firm intention at the date of the notice to develop the notice land, and is not just speculating or land-banking. Except in cases where planning permission is deemed (for example under a General Development Order or an Act of Parliament), planning permission is required. However, the wording of Case B does not require full or detailed planning permission. Outline planning permission may be sufficient, even if it is subject to reserved matters.[35] A permission in outline establishes outright the principle of the proposed development and it runs with the land. Once it grants it, the planning authority cannot go back on it other than by the process of formal revocation or modification, which may entitle the developer to compensation. A subsequent approval of reserved matters does not constitute a planning permission. It is merely an ancillary procedure by which the outline permission is made effective. The view that an outline permission suffices for the purposes of Case B also makes sense if one has regard to practice in the world of property development where, except in the case of a minor development, the making of an application in detail is rare.

Although Case B does not itself contain or express any time limit, the word 'required' may arguably (commentators differ) carry an element of timing, meaning that the landlord must be able to establish that she is able to implement the planning permission or develop at the date when the Notice expires, or within some reasonable time thereafter. But the latter – if it really is a part of the statutory test at all – is only in the sense that, if the likely commencement of the development is too far in the future, this may then cast doubt on whether the landlord

---

35 See the discussion by Lord Gill in *The Trustees of the North Berwick Trust v James B Miller & Co* [2009] CSIH 15 at Paras [22] and following.

really has the necessary intention to develop.

The only reported decision on the point of which I am aware is Windsor-Clive v Rees [2020] EWHC 2986 (Ch) where one of the grounds of the tenant's appeal against an arbitration award upholding a Case B Notice to Quit was an allegedly erroneous approach by the arbitrator to the words 'is required'. However, this ground of appeal had fallen away by the time of the hearing. HHJ Jarman QC, sitting as a judge of the High Court, said:

> "The key part of Case B in the present appeal is the phrase "is required." It was ultimately not in dispute before me that that means that the land must be so required at the end of the period stated in the notice or within a relatively short time thereafter, rather than in the more distant future or at some as yet unascertained time (see Jones v Gates [1954] 1 WLR 222 at 224 [...] It is also common ground that the landlords must show an intention to develop and a reasonable prospect of doing so (see Paddock Investments Ltd v Lory [1975] 2 EGLR 5)."

Even if 'a reasonable time' is required, what it is will depend on the circumstances of the case, including the nature of the development. The timing of a Case B Notice to Quit (not too soon, and not too late) can therefore be an issue requiring close thought.

Other tricky issues can arise in relation to Case B: for example, whether it captures a case where a landlord seeks to recover possession for both non-agricultural and agricultural purposes,[36] or where a planning permission authorises (for example) the development of a housing estate with 'green', or non-built elements such as 'wildflower meadows' (not intended to be used for grazing, and not intended to

---

36 See the decision of the Court of Appeal in *Floyer-Acland v Osmond* [2000] 2 EGLR 1

produce a grass crop), allotment gardens, woodland etc.

## Case C: Bad husbandry

**Not more than six months before the notice to quit, the Agricultural Land Tribunal granted a certificate of bad husbandry.**

The recovery of possession under this Special Case is begun by the landlord applying to the Tribunal that the Tribunal should certify that the tenant is not farming in accordance with the rules of good husbandry.

Those rules are set out in section 11 of the Agriculture Act 1947, and are implied into all 1986 Act tenancies.

Key amongst the rules of good husbandry is the tenant's obligation *'to maintain a reasonable standard of efficient production, as respects both the kind of produce and the quality and quantity thereof, while keeping the unit in a condition to enable such a standard to be maintained in the future...'.*

Before deciding whether to issue a certificate, the Tribunal will visit the holding so as to assess its general state and condition.

Until fairly recently, there was a widely-held view that Case C was genuinely useful only where agricultural use of the holding, or a significant part of it, had been all but abandoned.

Those were cases like Phillips v Davies (2007) which concerned 38 acres of land in Pembrokeshire. 10 acres had been abandoned, and parts of two fields had been used for dumping and burying scrap metal and other non-agricultural waste. A 2.5 acre field had a long-term dock problem. 12.5 acres/38 acres = about a third of the tenanted land. The Tribunal granted a certificate, and was upheld by the High Court on appeal: [2007] EWHC 1395 (Admin).

Another was <u>Tarmac UK v Hughes</u> (2009) which concerned two acres with a farmhouse which was a complete mess. Even though the management of the tenancy by the landlord had been woefully inadequate because they had not taken steps for 15 years to enforce the tenant's husbandry obligations, nonetheless, the landlord's failure had no effect on the tenant's ability to discharge his obligations of good husbandry. The Tribunal granted a certificate.

However, some – more recent – cases suggest that the approach of the Tribunal may be changing, with an increased emphasis on the long-term efficiency and economic viability of the holding, leading to certificates of bad husbandry perhaps being easier to obtain than in the past.

Treating 'efficiency' an important word, some (albeit not all) recent cases in the Tribunal on bad husbandry have emphasised the underlying statutory purpose – to make sure that farms with tenants who enjoy the protection of the 1986 Act (effective lifetime security of tenure) actually keep the farm up and farm efficiently.

In <u>Yorke v Barron</u> (2017) the Tribunal identified serious under-stocking of a 300 acre dairy holding, with a farm business being propped up by cottage rents and horse sales. What should have been a dairy or beef producing livestock was farm was neither. The farming was minimal with no discernible farming system. The horse sales were not a mere adjunct to a productive farm, but had become the core activities. The Tribunal granted a certificate of bad husbandry.

<u>Chapman v Lumb</u> (2015) was, to some degree, the converse. The Tribunal identified serious over-stocking, with not enough cubicles, and inadequate arrangements for feed, with poor stock-management, and significant long-term disrepair and lack of maintenance. The Tribunal granted a certificate.

To my mind, the focus on efficiency and maintaining agricultural production reflects more than different tribunals coming to different conclusions about marginal cases, and rather is reflective of an overall 'direction of travel' for the 1986 Act[37], because agricultural land is a scarce and valuable resource. This is foreshadowed in incoming legislation. For example, from 2024, the English Tribunal, when considering applications to succeed to agricultural tenancies, will have to consider the applicants "likely capability and capacity to farm the holding commercially, with or without other land, taking into account the need for high standards of efficient production an care for the environment in relation to managing that holding."[38]

But, even this is open to some doubt, because the desire to increase efficiency and production is not necessarily compatible with environmental objectives and 'greening'. There may be difficult cases where the two are in conflict.

If the Tribunal grants a certificate of bad husbandry, and the landlord issues a Notice to Quit on the back of it, then the tenant's legal recourse is very limited. If intending to continue to resist possession, then the tenant can either wait for the landlord to issue possession proceedings in court, which the tenant can then defend on the basis that the reason stated cannot be established, or can issue proceedings seeking a declaration that the Notice is invalid. Both these are tactics of last resort, and a tenant would have to reflect carefully as to whether the potential cost of such court proceedings (where, under the Civil Procedure Rules, costs are at large, and may well follow the event) would genuinely justify the steps.

---

37 And indeed the overall legislative apporach, post-Brexit, with its increased emphasis on domestic 'food security'.

38 See *The Agricultural Holdings ... (Suitability Test) (England) Regulations 2021*: SI 2021/619 Reg 5(2)

## Case D: Rent, and Remediable Breach of covenant

This is divided into two sub-cases.

**At the date of the giving of the notice to quit, the tenant has failed to comply with either (a) a Notice to pay rent due or (b) a Notice to remedy a remediable breach.**

The recovery of possession by the landlord under Case D is a notice-based system. This means that a successful Case D Notice to Quit is based entirely on the tenant's failure to comply with a relevant earlier notice to pay rent due or notice to remedy a remediable breach. If the tenant has failed to comply with the relevant earlier notice, then the question of whether the rent was ever actually paid, or whether the breach was ever actually remedied, are not relevant.

Given the importance of the notices to pay rent due or remedy a remediable breach, there are very strict requirements as to the wording and service of such notices. There are statutory forms. A Notice to Pay Rent or a Notice to Remedy Breach must be in the form prescribed by the Agricultural Holdings (Notices to Pay Rent or Remedy) Regulations 1987 (SI 1987/711). That is mandatory. Hence, a failure to use the correct form will render the whole exercise invalid. The statutory forms are to be found in the Schedule to the Regulations: Form 1 is for rent; Form 2 is a notice to remedy breaches where the remedy is doing work of repair, maintenance or replacement; Form 3 is a notice to remedy breaches 'not being a notice requiring the doing of any work of repair, maintenance or replacement'.

There are important 'Act Now' and other statutorily prescribed Notes which must also be included. Punctilious compliance with the statutory forms is required.

Compliance with the Notice to Pay Rent is all that really matters. If the tenant pays, but does so after the two months provided for by the standard form, then, although the rent is no longer owed, the tenant has nonetheless failed to comply with the Notice to Pay Rent, and the landlord is entitled to give a Case D Notice to Quit.[39]

It should be clear that tenants who receive notices to pay rent are well-advised to comply with them, immediately, and regardless of any arguments (for example) that the tenant has already paid, or is not liable to pay because convention is that the rent is paid at the annual tenant's dinner, or because the tenant thinks he is entitled to set off rent against a landlord's obligation to him, or because the amount of rent said to be due is said to be wrongly stated.

Non-compliance with a Notice to Pay Rent is a very high-risk strategy since it leaves the tenant with only one line of defence against the possession proceedings which will inevitably follow, which is that the notice to pay was not valid on common law grounds (e.g., vagueness).

Remediable breaches are breaches of covenants which are regarded (as a matter of law) as capable of being remedied. Frequently-encountered examples include breaches of covenants to reside in the farmhouse, or to use the farmhouse as a private dwelling only (this could, for example, technically be broken if the tenant used part of the farmhouse as the farm office). Irremediable breaches are dealt with under Case E: see below.

A Notice to Do Works (Form 2) and A Notice to remedy breach not doing works (Form 3) each give notice to remedy within a period set down by the landlord.

A challenge to a Notice to Do Works (Form 2) is by way of a demand for arbitration, in the one-month timescale, followed by an

---

[39] This is the effect of the decision of the Court of Appeal in *Stoneman v Brown* [1973] 1 WLR 459. There was no defence to the claim for possession.

arbitration. The 1986 Act gives the tenant a lifeline: even if a Notice to Quit based on the tenant's failure to comply with a Form 2 notice is upheld at arbitration, the tenant may still (within one month after the award) give a counter-notice invoking the Tribunal's jurisdiction. The landlord must then apply to the Tribunal for consent to the operation of his notice to quit. The Tribunal must consent unless it appears to them, having regard to the extent to which the tenant has failed to comply with the notice to do work, the consequences of his failure to comply with the notice in any respect, and the circumstances surrounding any such failure, that a fair and reasonable landlord would not insist on possession: AHA 1986 section 28(5).

Neither a Form 1 (Notice to Pay) or a Form 3 (notice to remedy breach not doing works) can be referred to arbitration until a later notice to quit is served on the ground that the tenant failed to comply with an earlier Notice to Pay or Form 3 notice.

Unlike Form 2, if the tenant fails to successfully challenge a Notice to Quit based on a Form 3 notice to remedy at arbitration, there is no role for the Tribunal.

## Case E: Remediable Breach

**At the date of the notice, the landlord's interest has been materially prejudiced by an irremediable breach of any term or condition of the tenancy agreement, by the tenant, which is not inconsistent with the tenant's duty to farm in accordance with the rules of good husbandry.**

Irremediable breaches are breaches of covenants which are regarded – as a matter of law – as incapable of being remedied. These are less common than remediable breaches, which are dealt with under Case D. The most frequently-encountered example of an irremediable breach is an assignment or sub-letting in breach of covenant.

The landlord must be able to demonstrate that the landlord's interest has been *"materially prejudiced"* by the breach. This is undefined, but a sound approach is that the breach has got to have a material adverse impact on the reversion. What is 'material' may depend on the circumstances of the case. Moreover, the breach which is alleged to have taken place should be "not inconsistent" with the tenant's duties in respect of good husbandry (see above).

Challenge to a Case E Notice is by way of a demand for arbitration, in the one-month timescale, followed by an arbitration.

**Case F: Insolvency**

**The tenant has become insolvent.**

'Insolvent' is defined in section 96(2) of the 1986 Act. For an individual, it means adjudged bankrupt, or entered into an Individual Voluntary Agreement. For a corporate body, it means wound-up or subject to a resolution to wind up. There are obvious gaps in the legislation (not least insofar as it fails to make mention of the Insolvency Act 1986).

This potentially offers a relatively quick and straightforward way of recovering possession. However, the change in the 'bankruptcy limit' (increased in 2015 from £750 to £5000) has inevitably discouraged landlords from issuing a Statutory Demand (which, if not met, could then be used as a springboard to petition for the tenant's bankruptcy) unless they are owed more than £5,000.

Of course, rent owing of less than £5,000 – even £1 – is still capable of being the subject of a Notice to Pay Rent which, if not complied with within the two months allowed, will found an incontestable Case D Notice to Quit.

But, if available, Case F is nonetheless very useful to the landlord because the general rule in section 25 that a notice to quit an agricultural holding has to give at least 12 months expiring on the term date does not apply where the tenant is insolvent (s.25(2)(a)), meaning that the landlord can give shorter notice.

Any challenge to a Case F notice has to be in court, either by way of defending the landlord's claim to possession, or bringing a claim for a declaration that the Case F notice is invalid, but bearing in mind the comments above – see Case C – as to the advisability of such a course of action.

## Case G: Tenant's death

**The tenant has died and less than three months has passed since the landlord received relevant notice.**

The tenant's death does not bring the tenancy to an end. It vests in the personal representatives.

'The relevant notice' to the landlord referred to in Case G can be either written notice from the personal representatives (for which there is no prescribed form) or service on the landlord of an application for a succession tenancy (which must be made within three months of the tenant's death).

In the absence of 'relevant notice', time will not begin to run against the landlord for the purposes of the landlord's Case G notice, even if he happens to know of the tenant's death (for example, if he carried the tenant's coffin at the funeral).[40]

In the case of an intestate tenant, written notice has to come from the

---

40 See, for example, *Lees v Tatchell* [1990] 1 EGLR 10

personal representatives. Therefore, it cannot be given before letters of administration have been obtained.

If the tenant died testate, the personal representatives derive their authority from the will and notification to the landlord at any time after the death by those persons will start time running.

If a succession application is made, then the landlord applies to the Tribunal for consent to the operation of a Case G notice to quit.

## Case H: Minister's certificate

**Restructuring or reshaping of agricultural units.**

This Special Case is only available to the Secretary of State. You are unlikely to encounter one (I never have). If you do, consult one of the standard practitioners' works, or seek specialist advice.

# CHAPTER FOUR

# SUCCESSION TO A 1986 ACT TENANCY

Succession is a very important feature of some tenancies under the 1986 Act. But rights to apply to succeed to an AHT generally exist only where (i) the tenancy was first granted before 12th July 1984, or (ii) if the tenancy was first granted between 12 July 1984 and 1 September 1995, the parties expressly contracted into the succession provisions of the 1986 Act, or (iii) the tenancy itself is a (first) successor tenancy.

Succession rights are potentially exercisable on up to two occasions, on the tenant's death or retirement. The provisions relating to succession on death and on retirement are broadly similar.

## Succession applications to the Tribunal on the death of the tenant

The aspirant successor must make an application to the Tribunal within 3 months of the date of death. **Time is of the essence.** This deadline is strict and cannot be extended by the Tribunal. For that reason, it is wise to try to avoid last-minute applications, even if doing so is tempting because (for example) there are discussions between the prospective successor and the landlord. The fact of ongoing discussions, no matter how cordial and productive, does not exempt the applicant from applying to the Tribunal in time. If the applicant does not apply within three months, and negotiations break down, then the applicant is left in real jeopardy.

Use the appropriate Tribunal form (available online) but note that the Tribunal in England and the Tribunal in Wales use different forms. Notice should also be given to the landlord (not least, because the making of an application to succeed starts the landlord's clock running to give a Case G Notice to Quit). The aspirant successor should attach as much supporting information to the form as she can. But the most important thing is to file the application form on time. That should not be put on hold whilst supporting paperwork is assembled. With the Tribunal's permission, that can be provided later.

If the landlord wishes to oppose the application, or comment on it, she must complete and return to the Tribunal the appropriate form within the timescale set down by the Rules.

The landlord can also resist a succession application by issuing a Case G notice, and then applying to the Tribunal for consent to its operation. If this happens, then the Tribunal will (usually) first determine the application to succeed before going on to determine whether the landlord's Case G notice should have effect.

An aspirant successor must prove to the Tribunal that she is both 'eligible' and 'suitable'.

Both concepts can present difficulties for applicants. The 1986 Act is now perhaps showing its age. The legislation was better suited to a model of farms and farming where the farm was economically self-sufficient – in the sense that the farm income was both sufficient to support the farming family (without the need for anyone to work elsewhere) and came entirely from the production of food (and not from activities off the farm, or diversified activities on the farm). These remarks are especially relevant when it comes to consider whether the applicant satisfies the 'livelihood' condition, which is an element of eligibility.

## Eligibility

Eligibility is technical, and can be arbitrary.

### *Close relative*

The applicant must be a 'close relative' of the deceased tenant. This is defined by the 1986 Act as meaning a spouse or civil partner, a sibling, a child (including step or adopted children) or "any person (not being a sibling or a child) who, in the case of any marriage or civil partnership to which the deceased was at any time a party, was treated by the deceased as a child of the family in relation to that marriage or civil partnership."

There are obvious omissions from this list, such as grandchildren, nephews, and nieces. They are not 'close relatives', as defined, and therefore are not eligible to apply to succeed and cannot do so. The Tribunal has no power or discretion to consider an application by someone who is not a close relative. If that person wishes to take a tenancy, then they will have to try to negotiate a solution with the landlord.

There are other anomalies. For example, where two siblings (one with children, one childless) hold the tenancy as joint tenants, and survivorship operates, whether any of the children can apply to succeed on the death or retirement of the surviving joint tenant depends on which sibling dies first. If the sibling with children dies first, the tenancy survives to the unmarried sibling, and the nieces and nephews are not his close relatives and cannot apply. If the childless sibling dies first, then the tenancy survives to the parent sibling, and the children are eligible to apply. The scenario is so common as to be popularly (but inaccurately) known as 'the bachelor trap'.

## The 'livelihood condition'

The second part of eligibility is the livelihood condition.

The Applicant must satisfy the Tribunal that '*in the seven years ending with the date of death*' (of the former tenant) the applicant's '*only or principal source of livelihood throughout a continuous period of not less than five years, or two or more discontinuous period together amounting to not less than five years, derived from his agricultural work on the holding or on an agricultural unit of which the holding forms part*': AHA 1986 section 36(3)(a)

This is often the main battleground in disputed applications by a close relative to succeed to the tenancy.

There are several issues to consider. The first is the proper meaning of 'agricultural work'. Manual work on the farm (milking etc) should straightforwardly qualify. Qualifying work probably includes work which is closely connected with the agricultural activity on the holding, but which is not actually done on the farm, such as agricultural contracting (using the farm's equipment to cut hedges etc for other farmers) or cattle-dealing. It may also catch work which contributes to the agricultural activity but which is 'white collar' rather than muddy boots (for instance, keeping the farm's books and records).

More challenging scenarios can arise where the applicant has worked on the farm, but this work has been part of a diversified enterprise such as running a farm shop, or a B&B in the farmhouse. Such work does not (at least on the face of it) fall squarely within the definition of 'agriculture' given in section 96 of the Act, which has to be met if the tenancy is to be the tenancy of an *agricultural* holding. Whilst some legislative tinkering in 2006[41] allowed such work to qualify for

---

41 *The Regulatory Reform (Agricultural Tenancies) (England and Wales) Order*

the purposes of the livelihood condition if the landlord had approved of it in writing, there is no compulsion on a landlord to do so, and it is not obvious why (except for philanthropy) a landlord would want to do so voluntarily.

'*Principal*' just means 'more than half': 50.01% would be good enough. 49.99% would not be good enough.

'*Livelihood*' can prove to be a difficult and controversial issue. In the leading case, Casswell v Welby [1995] 71 P & CR 137, the Court of Appeal said that livelihood was to be defined as *'means of living, that is to say what is spent or consumed for the purpose of living. The source of one's livelihood insofar as it is money is income; insofar as it is the use or consumption of goods, it is benefits in kind'*. An applicant may have income derived from one or more sources. If so, in order to qualify, the income derived from work on the agricultural holding must be greater than the income from other sources.

The Court of Appeal was clear that section 36(3)(a) was to be construed in a purposive manner, as a jury would do, and without adopting too legalistic an approach. The section simply requires the Applicant to establish their economic dependence on the holding by showing that their work on the holding provided their main means of livelihood.

Despite this guidance, parties nonetheless do sometimes spend a lot of time, effort, and money in a forensic dissection of the applicant's livelihood, in the attempt either (on the part of the applicant) to reach a figure of over 50% (even marginally) for 5 of 7 years, or (on the part of the landlord) to drive the figure down to less (even marginally) than 50% for 3 of 7 years. The Tribunal has itself also, on occasion, been tempted by such efforts, engaging in complex calculations (for

---

*2006*, SI 2006/2805

example) as to the value of the applicant's bed and board in the farmhouse as opposed to living and eating elsewhere. But parties should reflect on whether such detailed effort reflects the guidance of the Court of Appeal, and whether it is genuinely justified in cases where livelihood, one way or the other, and even on a broad-brush basis, seems fairly clear.

Further complexity is potentially introduced by the issue of resources other than the applicant's. On one view, this is irrelevant: the livelihood test, as set out in the statute, applies only to the applicant for succession, and to no-one else. When it comes to the income of an applicant's spouse or civil partner, it is to be noted that section 36(3)(a) is not an income test, let alone a 'joint income' test. Casswell v Welby itself touches on some of these issues, but it cannot be said for sure that questions as to whether the income or livelihood of an applicant's spouse or civil partner, or the generosity or benevolence of relatives, are always irrelevant.

Here, but only in the event of applications to succeed on the *death* of the tenant (and not in the event of applications to succeed on the tenant's retirement) section 41 of the 1986 Act provides an important degree of latitude when it comes to assessing the applicant's livelihood. Where an applicant is otherwise, and in all respects, an eligible person, but the source of livelihood test, although not fully satisfied, is satisfied to "a material extent", and it would be fair and reasonable to treat him or her as fully eligible, then the applicant can apply to be treated as fully eligible.

This has to be specifically applied for on the application form. If it is not so applied for, the Tribunal may not be able to consider it. So, and even if you are sure that you will comfortably satisfy the livelihood condition, tick the box!

What is 'a material extent' is a matter of fact and degree. This may depend on whether the failure to meet the livelihood condition was a 'near' miss or not, both in terms of years, and in terms of percentage. As to the latter, the gist of the Tribunal's reported decisions is that something in the region of 40% in any of the seven years which fail to exceed 50% is required. Something significantly less than 40% may fail, on the facts, to satisfy the Tribunal.

The statute gives no further guidance as to what is 'fair and reasonable'. This has to be a matter of fact and degree.

## Not an occupier of a commercial unit.

The third element of eligibility, which must be satisfied, is that the applicant must not be in occupation of a commercial unit of agricultural land: section 36(3)(b). The gist of this condition – perhaps reflecting an old-fashioned notion of dynastic farming, with prospective successors staying to work on the farm rather than spreading their wings and going elsewhere – is that a successor has to be economically dependent on their work on *this* holding; and, if they occupy a suitably sized holding elsewhere, capable of supporting them economically, then they will be expected to make their living from that.

A 'commercial unit' is "*a unit of agricultural land which is capable when farmed under competent management of producing a net annual income of an amount not less than the aggregate of the average annual earning of two full-time male agricultural workers, aged 20 or over.*"

There are some complicated rules about this in Schedule 6 of the 1986 Act, and the circumstances in which an applicant is deemed to be in occupation of other land for the purposes of this test.

When an application to succeed to an agricultural tenancy is made, the Tribunals' forms ask the landlord whether the landlord wants a 'Net Annual Income Assessment' to be conducted. This is sometimes referred to as a 'Minister's assessment.' Any Net Annual Income Assessment is performed by the Tribunal (actually, by a specialist appointed and paid for by the Tribunal). It will look at the other land (that is, apart from the holding) which the applicant has declared that she occupies. If the applicant has not declared that they occupy any land other than the holding, then asking for a Net Annual Income Assessment will be pointless, and the Tribunal is unlikely to order one to be conducted, unless the landlord has some decent evidential basis for saying that the applicant is in occupation of other land, but has failed to declare it. If that is the case, the landlord should raise this clearly with the Tribunal. Even then, if an applicant is in occupation of (say) 50 acres of rough upland grazing off the holding, that is unlikely to amount to a commercial unit.

This is because the purpose of the Assessment is to assess any other land occupied by the applicant, so as to establish its 'productive capacity'. The calculation of the productive capacity is done on the basis of the figures set out annually in the Schedule to Agricultural Holdings (Units of Production) Order. This is a statutory instrument. England and Wales have different orders. The Assessment will produce a figure, and the commercial unit test will be met, or not met.

## Suitability

Having dealt with eligibility, the Tribunal must also be satisfied that the applicant is, 'in their opinion', 'a suitable person to become the tenant of the holding'. The suitability test is free-standing from eligibility, and it is certainly possible for an eligible applicant nonetheless not to be suitable to become tenant.

In assessing suitability, section 39(8) of the 1986 Act directs the Tribunal to 'have regard to all relevant matters including (a) the extent to which the applicant has been trained in, or had practical experience of, agriculture; (b) the age, physical health and financial standing of the applicant; and (c) the views (if any) stated by the landlord on the applicant's suitability.

The legal and evidential burden of satisfying the Tribunal is on the Applicant, who must collect and put forward sufficient evidence to satisfy the Tribunal that the Applicant is suitable.

It is to be noted that the statutory factors are not exhaustive. Something sometimes encountered is an applicant who has criminal convictions. These may be potentially relevant (for example, disqualification from driving on the public roads may affect an applicant's ability to get from one part of the holding to another) although the Act is careful to describe the test as one of suitability and not one of moral character.

The Tribunal has a wide discretion. Here, it has to be borne in mind that the Tribunal is usually made up of a panel of three people – a legally qualified chair, sitting with a farmer and a landowner. As such, overly legalistic approaches to the issue of suitability – for example, attempts to require the applicant to demonstrate access to capital reserves as part of their financial standing – may not be the most effective.

There is a general consensus that the Tribunal will overall take a common-sense approach, looking to the statutory factors, and then standing back and asking the general question as to whether the applicant is someone who will pay the rent and keep the farm in good condition.

If an applicant satisfies the Tribunal that she is both eligible and suitable, then (unless the landlord has served a Case G Special Case Notice, and can gain the Tribunal's consent its operation) the Tribunal <u>must</u> make a direction entitling the applicant to the grant of a new tenancy, the terms of which will be the same as the terms of the old tenancy.

## Succession applications to the Tribunal on the retirement of the tenant

These are less frequently encountered than applications to succeed on death. Such applications are potentially deterred by two quirks of the rules.

The first quirk is that section 41 of the 1986 Act does not apply to applications to succeed on retirement. Therefore, in retirement cases, the applicant has to satisfy the livelihood condition full-stop, and there is no 'material extent' fall-back.

The second quirk is that an unsuccessful application for succession on retirement bars the same person from later applying to succeed on the tenant's death.[42]

The rules as to eligibility and suitability are otherwise the same as for applications to succeed on death.

The tenant has to give a retirement notice, and either has to have reached the age of 65 at the date the retirement notice takes effect, or must be permanently physically or mentally incapacitated at that date. The retirement notice has to take effect on the term date at least 12 months from the date of the notice. It must contain the nomination of one person, eligible within the meaning of the Act, as successor. It is not possible to nominate more than one person.

---

42 AHA 1986, section 53

# CHAPTER FIVE

# DISPUTE RESOLUTION

## The Resolution of Disputes outside the Tribunal

In relation to FBTs under the 1995 Act, section 28 provides that any dispute between the landlord and tenant under an FBT concerning their rights and obligations under the 1995 Act, 'shall be determined by arbitration'. However, there are exceptions. Section 29 provides that an FBT can contain its own dispute resolution mechanism, therefore overriding section 28.

The 1986 Act provides that many matters of dispute have to be referred to arbitration. Some have been discussed above – for example, Schedule 1 matters, and certain sorts of Special Case Notices to Quit. There are others, such as compensation for fixed equipment, rent review, and settlement of certain claims at the end of the tenancy.

Arbitrations are governed by the Arbitration Act 1996. Section 1 sets out the object of arbitration, which is to obtain the fair resolution of disputes by an impartial tribunal without unnecessary delay or expense, adopting procedures (for example, about evidence, documents, and submissions) which are suitable to the circumstances of the particular case.

Despite these aims, it should not be assumed that arbitration is invariably a quick and straightforward way of resolving the dispute, or even that it will be quicker and more straightforward than going to court.

An important matter to be considered before embarking on arbitration are the potential costs, and the potential incidence of those costs. Arbitrations can be expensive. In contrast to court proceedings, where the judge is paid for through general taxation, the arbitrator will charge the parties a professional fee for their services. Non-lawyer arbitrators sometimes appoint legal advisers or assessors to advise the arbitrator as to legal aspects of the dispute, and this adviser/assessor will also be entitled to charge a professional fee for their services.

The arbitrator may make an award allocating the costs of the arbitration – which are the arbitrator's fees and expenses, the fees and expenses of any arbitral institution concerned, and the legal or other costs of the parties – as between the parties. Unless the parties otherwise agree, the arbitrator shall award costs on the general principle that costs should follow the event except where it appears to the arbitrator that in the circumstances it is not appropriate in relation to the whole or part of the costs: section 61 of the Arbitration Act 1996.

The second aspect is complexity. Except for location and the absence of wigs and gowns, arbitrations can sometimes be indistinguishable from a fully-fledged conventional court case, with witnesses giving oral evidence, and that oral evidence being tested by way of cross-examination.

These factors gave rise to significant and well-publicised criticism of the general operation of the Arbitration Act. In response to this, Schedule 4 of Deregulation Act 2015 now provides that disputes – except in relation to Notices to Quit, which remain the province of the arbitrator, or the Tribunal, as the case may be – can also be resolved by 'third party determination' rather than by arbitration. Third party determination is therefore a possibility, but the rules and governing principles are unclear, and seem to be largely (if not entirely) in the hands of the parties.

The third party must be appointed in writing. It is obvious that great care will have to be taken in drafting such an agreement, since the relationship between the parties and the third party, the third party's obligations, and the circumstances in which the decision will be final and/or binding on the parties will need to be governed by the terms of the contract. It would be most unfortunate if the parties, having appointed a third party, then had to go to Court to elicit the meaning of their agreement. Unlike arbitration, the procedure to be adopted is not automatically governed by statute. Hence, unless the parties seek to adopt and incorporate, 'off-the-peg', a ready-made code (such as, for example, the Arbitration Act) then they are thrown to their own resources.

Third Party Determination is very different to arbitration. It is subject to very little review or intervention by the court. The third party is not a judge, and is not performing a judicial function. The process (whatever the parties agree it should be) leads to a 'determination', and not to an award or a judgment. Unless the parties agree otherwise, there is no right of appeal.

It is not entirely clear whether a determination could be impeached – for instance, if the third party arrived at a determination on a fundamentally erroneous and demonstrable factual basis. The most careful approach would be to expressly provide for the grounds of challenge in the TPD contract: e.g., departure from instructions; exceeding the agreed ambit of the determination; or manifest error of fact (or, perhaps, error of law).

## Dispute Resolution in the Tribunal

The following remarks are intended to be general guidance to those who need to deal with the Tribunals.

### Forms:

1. Use the Tribunal's website to find out whether there is a particular form which should be used (there usually will be).

2. If a form is in PDF format, and you do not have a programme such as Adobe Acrobat DC or PDF Expert 7 which allows you to fill it in, ask the Tribunal if it has a form in Word or some other editable format.

3. If the Tribunal does not have a form in a format which you can complete on a computer, print off the form, complete it by hand, and either scan it and email it back, or put it in the post.

4. If putting a form in the post, copy or take a photo of the whole form for your records. Do not rely on the Tribunal later being able to supply you with copies of what you have sent.

5. If time is of the essence (it often is) then use recorded delivery and/or get a certificate of posting to avoid disputes about timing.

## Writing to the Tribunal:

6. The Tribunal manages a caseload. Whenever you correspond with the Tribunal, put the case details (eg names, and land) and number (if you have one) clearly at the top of your email or letter.

7. Always identify on whose behalf you are writing (eg, 'I am the Applicant', or 'I am the Applicant's solicitor'). Do not leave the Tribunal to have to work it out.

8. Whenever you write, copy your letter to the other party(ies), and make it clear on your letter or email that you have done so (eg, 'I am copying this email to all the other parties: you will see their email addresses are in the copy to box above). The Tribunal has to deal openly and transparently with the parties, and cannot correspond with one party without being confident that all parties are seeing the correspondence.

9. The Tribunal's staff are civil servants and are entitled to respect in the workplace. Be courteous in all your dealings with them.

10. Write only when you really have a good purpose. Write in terms which are as simple and straightforward as you can. Know what you are asking for, and why. Do not leave the Tribunal to have to try to puzzle it out.

## Your case:

11. The Tribunal is an independent judicial body and cannot give you legal advice.

12. If the Tribunal writes to you with directions for the management of your case, the directions are orders, and not suggestions, and must be complied with.

13. If you cannot comply with a direction in time, contact the Tribunal, preferably in advance of the date, explain the situation, and ask for more time. Open-ended requests for more time are less likely to be favourably received than those which set out a realistic timescale.

14. Tribunal's letters, if dealing with a substantive matter, and even if signed by a Tribunal official, are often drafted by a judge, and may contain valuable guidance as to further steps.

## Hearings:

15. The Tribunal's hearings are normally held in public, and not in private.

16. Expect a panel of three – a legally-qualified chairperson and two (usually, not legally qualified) 'wingers' – usually a 'farmer' member and a 'landowner' member.

17. Site visits and inspections are an important fact-finding part of many of the Tribunal's cases (and are, formally, a part of the hearing).

18. The Tribunal is an adversarial jurisdiction: it decides the cases which are brought to it and answers the questions which it is

asked to answer. The evidence which the parties choose to advance is, by and large, a matter of choice for the parties, albeit subject to control by the Tribunal. The Tribunal is not an inquisitorial jurisdiction and does not have mandate to engage in detective work.

# APPENDIX A

# SUGGESTED FURTHER READING

Halsbury's Laws of England, Volume 1 – 'Agricultural Law and Allotments' (5th edition, 2018, ed. C McNall)

Muir Watt and Moss, 'Agricultural Holdings' (15th edition, 2018, ed Sir T Fancourt and others)

Christopher Rodgers, Agricultural Law (4th edition, 2016)

Scammell Densham and Williams (10th edition, 2015 with First Supplement, 2018, ed P R Williams) 'The Law of Agricultural Holdings'

# APPENDIX B

# USEFUL ADDRESSES AND CONTACT DETAILS

Agricultural Land Tribunal for Wales

Agricultural Land Tribunal Wales
Welsh Tribunals Unit
PO Box 100
Llandrindod Wells
Powys
LD1 9BW
http://agriculturallandtribunal.gov.wales
Email: agriculturallandtribunal@gov.wales
Phone: 0300 025 9809

Agricultural Land Tribunal for England

First-tier Tribunal (Property Chamber)
Agricultural Land and Drainage
1st Floor, Piccadilly Exchange
Piccadilly Plaza
Manchester
M1 4AH
Email: aldgeneralenquiries@justice.gov.uk
Phone: 0161 237 9491
Fax: 01264 785 128

## Agricultural Law Association

Office 1
The Stackyard
Bulwick
Northamptonshire
NN17 3DY
http://ala.org.uk
Email:   enquiries@ala.org.uk

# MORE BOOKS BY LAW BRIEF PUBLISHING

A selection of our other titles available now:-

| |
|---|
| 'A Practical Guide to Parental Alienation in Private and Public Law Children Cases' by Sam King QC & Frankie Shama |
| 'Contested Heritage – Removing Art from Land and Historic Buildings' by Richard Harwood QC, Catherine Dobson, David Sawtell |
| 'The Limits of Separate Legal Personality: When Those Running a Company Can Be Held Personally Liable for Losses Caused to Third Parties Outside of the Company' by Dr Mike Wilkinson |
| 'A Practical Guide to Transgender Law' by Robin Moira White & Nicola Newbegin |
| 'Artificial Intelligence – The Practical Legal Issues (2nd Edition)' by John Buyers |
| 'A Practical Guide to Residential Freehold Conveyancing' by Lorraine Richardson |
| 'A Practical Guide to Pensions on Divorce for Lawyers' by Bryan Scant |
| 'A Practical Guide to Challenging Sham Marriage Allegations in Immigration Law' by Priya Solanki |
| 'A Practical Guide to Legal Rights in Scotland' by Sarah-Jane Macdonald |
| 'A Practical Guide to New Build Conveyancing' by Paul Sams & Rebecca East |
| 'A Practical Guide to Defending Barristers in Disciplinary Cases' by Marc Beaumont |
| 'A Practical Guide to Inherited Wealth on Divorce' by Hayley Trim |
| 'A Practical Guide to Practice Direction 12J and Domestic Abuse in Private Law Children Proceedings' by Rebecca Cross & Malvika Jaganmohan |
| 'A Practical Guide to Confiscation and Restraint' by Narita Bahra QC, John Carl Townsend, David Winch |
| 'A Practical Guide to the Law of Forests in Scotland' by Philip Buchan |
| 'A Practical Guide to Health and Medical Cases in Immigration Law' by Rebecca Chapman & Miranda Butler |
| 'A Practical Guide to Bad Character Evidence for Criminal Practitioners by Aparna Rao |
| 'A Practical Guide to Extradition Law post-Brexit' by Myles Grandison et al |

| |
|---|
| 'A Practical Guide to Hoarding and Mental Health for Housing Lawyers' by Rachel Coyle |
| 'A Practical Guide to Psychiatric Claims in Personal Injury – 2nd Edition' by Liam Ryan |
| 'Stephens on Contractual Indemnities' by Richard Stephens |
| 'A Practical Guide to the EU Succession Regulation' by Richard Frimston |
| 'A Practical Guide to Solicitor and Client Costs – 2nd Edition' by Robin Dunne |
| 'Constructive Dismissal – Practice Pointers and Principles' by Benjimin Burgher |
| 'A Practical Guide to Religion and Belief Discrimination Claims in the Workplace' by Kashif Ali |
| 'A Practical Guide to the Law of Medical Treatment Decisions' by Ben Troke |
| 'Fundamental Dishonesty and QOCS in Personal Injury Proceedings: Law and Practice' by Jake Rowley |
| 'A Practical Guide to the Law in Relation to School Exclusions' by Charlotte Hadfield & Alice de Coverley |
| 'A Practical Guide to Divorce for the Silver Separators' by Karin Walker |
| 'The Right to be Forgotten – The Law and Practical Issues' by Melissa Stock |
| 'A Practical Guide to Planning Law and Rights of Way in National Parks, the Broads and AONBs' by James Maurici QC, James Neill et al |
| 'A Practical Guide to Election Law' by Tom Tabori |
| 'A Practical Guide to the Law in Relation to Surrogacy' by Andrew Powell |
| 'A Practical Guide to Claims Arising from Fatal Accidents – 2nd Edition' by James Patience |
| 'A Practical Guide to the Ownership of Employee Inventions – From Entitlement to Compensation' by James Tumbridge & Ashley Roughton |
| 'A Practical Guide to Asbestos Claims' by Jonathan Owen & Gareth McAloon |
| 'A Practical Guide to Stamp Duty Land Tax in England and Northern Ireland' by Suzanne O'Hara |
| 'A Practical Guide to the Law of Farming Partnerships' by Philip Whitcomb |
| 'Covid-19, Homeworking and the Law – The Essential Guide to Employment and GDPR Issues' by Forbes Solicitors |
| 'Covid-19 and Criminal Law – The Essential Guide' by Ramya Nagesh |
| 'Covid-19 and Family Law in England and Wales – The Essential Guide' by Safda Mahmood |

| |
|---|
| 'A Practical Guide to the Law of Unlawful Eviction and Harassment – 2nd Edition' by Stephanie Lovegrove |
| 'Covid-19, Brexit and the Law of Commercial Leases – The Essential Guide' by Mark Shelton |
| 'A Practical Guide to Costs in Personal Injury Claims – 2nd Edition' by Matthew Hoe |
| 'A Practical Guide to the General Data Protection Regulation (GDPR) – 2nd Edition' by Keith Markham |
| 'Ellis on Credit Hire – Sixth Edition' by Aidan Ellis & Tim Kevan |
| 'A Practical Guide to Working with Litigants in Person and McKenzie Friends in Family Cases' by Stuart Barlow |
| 'Protecting Unregistered Brands: A Practical Guide to the Law of Passing Off by Lorna Brazell |
| 'A Practical Guide to Secondary Liability and Joint Enterprise Post-Jogee' by Joanne Cecil & James Mehigan |
| 'A Practical Guide to the Pre-Action RTA Claims Protocol for Personal Injury Lawyers' by Antonia Ford |
| 'A Practical Guide to Neighbour Disputes and the Law' by Alexander Walsh |
| 'A Practical Guide to Forfeiture of Leases' by Mark Shelton |
| 'A Practical Guide to Coercive Control for Legal Practitioners and Victims' by Rachel Horman |
| 'A Practical Guide to Rights Over Airspace and Subsoil' by Daniel Gatty |
| 'Tackling Disclosure in the Criminal Courts – A Practitioner's Guide' by Narita Bahra QC & Don Ramble |
| 'A Practical Guide to the Law of Driverless Cars – Second Edition' by Alex Glassbrook, Emma Northey & Scarlett Milligan |
| 'A Practical Guide to TOLATA Claims' by Greg Williams |
| 'A Practical Guide to Elderly Law – 2nd Edition' by Justin Patten |
| 'A Practical Guide to Responding to Housing Disrepair and Unfitness Claims' by Iain Wightwick |
| 'A Practical Guide to the Construction and Rectification of Wills and Trust Instruments' by Edward Hewitt |
| 'A Practical Guide to the Law of Bullying and Harassment in the Workplace' by Philip Hyland |
| 'How to Be a Freelance Solicitor: A Practical Guide to the SRA-Regulated Freelance Solicitor Model' by Paul Bennett |

| |
|---|
| 'A Practical Guide to Prison Injury Claims' by Malcolm Johnson |
| 'A Practical Guide to the Small Claims Track - 2nd Edition' by Dominic Bright |
| 'A Practical Guide to Advising Clients at the Police Station' by Colin Stephen McKeown-Beaumont |
| 'A Practical Guide to Antisocial Behaviour Injunctions' by Iain Wightwick |
| 'Practical Mediation: A Guide for Mediators, Advocates, Advisers, Lawyers, and Students in Civil, Commercial, Business, Property, Workplace, and Employment Cases' by Jonathan Dingle with John Sephton |
| 'The Mini-Pupillage Workbook' by David Boyle |
| 'A Practical Guide to Crofting Law' by Brian Inkster |
| 'A Practical Guide to Spousal Maintenance' by Liz Cowell |
| 'A Practical Guide to the Law of Domain Names and Cybersquatting' by Andrew Clemson |
| 'A Practical Guide to the Law of Gender Pay Gap Reporting' by Harini Iyengar |
| 'A Practical Guide to the Rights of Grandparents in Children Proceedings' by Stuart Barlow |
| 'NHS Whistleblowing and the Law' by Joseph England |
| 'Employment Law and the Gig Economy' by Nigel Mackay & Annie Powell |
| 'A Practical Guide to Noise Induced Hearing Loss (NIHL) Claims' by Andrew Mckie, Ian Skeate, Gareth McAloon |
| 'An Introduction to Beauty Negligence Claims – A Practical Guide for the Personal Injury Practitioner' by Greg Almond |
| 'Intercompany Agreements for Transfer Pricing Compliance' by Paul Sutton |
| 'Zen and the Art of Mediation' by Martin Plowman |
| 'A Practical Guide to the SRA Principles, Individual and Law Firm Codes of Conduct 2019 – What Every Law Firm Needs to Know' by Paul Bennett |
| 'A Practical Guide to Adoption for Family Lawyers' by Graham Pegg |
| 'A Practical Guide to Industrial Disease Claims' by Andrew Mckie & Ian Skeate |
| 'A Practical Guide to Redundancy' by Philip Hyland |
| 'A Practical Guide to Vicarious Liability' by Mariel Irvine |
| 'A Practical Guide to Applications for Landlord's Consent and Variation of Leases' by Mark Shelton |
| 'A Practical Guide to Relief from Sanctions Post-Mitchell and Denton' by Peter Causton |

| |
|---|
| 'A Practical Guide to Equity Release for Advisors' by Paul Sams |
| 'A Practical Guide to Financial Services Claims' by Chris Hegarty |
| 'The Law of Houses in Multiple Occupation: A Practical Guide to HMO Proceedings' by Julian Hunt |
| 'Occupiers, Highways and Defective Premises Claims: A Practical Guide Post-Jackson – 2nd Edition' by Andrew Mckie |
| 'A Practical Guide to Financial Ombudsman Service Claims' by Adam Temple & Robert Scrivenor |
| 'A Practical Guide to Advising Schools on Employment Law' by Jonathan Holden |
| 'A Practical Guide to Running Housing Disrepair and Cavity Wall Claims: 2nd Edition' by Andrew Mckie & Ian Skeate |
| 'A Practical Guide to Holiday Sickness Claims – 2nd Edition' by Andrew Mckie & Ian Skeate |
| 'Arguments and Tactics for Personal Injury and Clinical Negligence Claims' by Dorian Williams |
| 'A Practical Guide to Drone Law' by Rufus Ballaster, Andrew Firman, Eleanor Clot |
| 'A Practical Guide to Compliance for Personal Injury Firms Working With Claims Management Companies' by Paul Bennett |
| 'RTA Allegations of Fraud in a Post-Jackson Era: The Handbook – 2nd Edition' by Andrew Mckie |
| 'RTA Personal Injury Claims: A Practical Guide Post-Jackson' by Andrew Mckie |
| 'On Experts: CPR35 for Lawyers and Experts' by David Boyle |
| 'An Introduction to Personal Injury Law' by David Boyle |

These books and more are available to order online direct from the publisher at www.lawbriefpublishing.com, where you can also read free sample chapters. For any queries, contact us on 0844 587 2383 or mail@lawbriefpublishing.com.

Our books are also usually in stock at www.amazon.co.uk with free next day delivery for Prime members, and at good legal bookshops such as Wildy & Sons.

We are regularly launching new books in our series of practical day-to-day practitioners' guides. Visit our website and join our free newsletter to be kept informed and to receive special offers, free chapters, etc.

You can also follow us on Twitter at www.twitter.com/lawbriefpub.

Printed in Great Britain
by Amazon